Church Basics

Understanding the Congregation's Authority

Author and Series Editor Jonathan Leeman

B&H
PUBLISHING GROUP
Nashville, Tennessee

978-1-4336-8893-5

Published by B&H Publishing Group
Nashville, Tennessee

Dewey Decimal Classification: 262
Subject Heading: CHURCH MEMBERSHIP \ CHURCH RENEWAL \
CHURCH GOVERNMENT AND POLITY

Unless otherwise noted, all Scripture is from the Holman Christian
Standard Bible (HCSB), copyright © 1999, 2000, 2002, 2003, 2009
by Holman Bible Publishers. Used by permission.

Also used: English Standard Version, (ESV) copyright © 2001 by Crossway
Bibles, a publishing ministry of Good News Publishers.
ESV Text Edition: 2007. All rights reserved.

1 2 3 4 5 6 7 8 • 20 19 18 17 16

CONTENTS

"Church member, did you know you have a job every bit as
important as the pastor's? This book explains what that is."
—Mark Dever

CHURCH BASICS SERIES PREFACE

The Christian life is the churched life. This basic biblical conviction informs every book in the Church Basics series.

That conviction in turn affects how each author treats his topic. For instance, the Lord's Supper is not a private, mystical act between you and Jesus. It is a meal around the family table in which you commune with Christ and Christ's people. The Great Commission is not a license to head into the nations as Jesus' witness all by oneself. It is a charge given to the whole church to be fulfilled by the whole church. The authority of the church rests not only with the leaders, but with the entire assembly. Every member has a job to do, including you.

Every book is written *for* the average church member, and this is a crucial point. If the Christian life is a churched life, then you, a baptized believer and church member, have a responsibility to understand these basic topics. Just as Jesus charges you with promoting and protecting his gospel message, so he charges you with promoting and protecting his gospel people, the church. These books will explain how.

You are like a shareholder in Christ's gospel ministry corporation. And what do good shareholders do? They study their company, study the market, and study the competition. They want the most out of their investment. You, Christian, have invested your whole life in the gospel. The purpose of the series, then, is to help you maximize the health and kingdom profitability of your local congregation for God's glorious gospel ends.

Are you ready to get to work?

Jonathan Leeman
Series Editor

Books in the Church Basics series:

Understanding the Great Commission, Mark Dever
Understanding Baptism, Bobby Jamieson
Understanding the Lord's Supper, Bobby Jamieson
Understanding the Congregation's Authority, Jonathan Leeman
Understanding Church Discipline, Jonathan Leeman
Understanding Church Leadership, Mark Dever

For further instruction on these topics from these authors (B&H Academic):

Don't Fire Your Church Members: The Case for Congregationalism, Jonathan Leeman

Going Public: Why Baptism Is Required for Church Membership, Bobby Jamieson

Baptist Foundations: Church Government for an Anti-Institutional Age, Mark Dever and Jonathan Leeman, editors

Preach: Theology Meets Practice, Mark Dever and Greg Gilbert

The Church: The Gospel Made Visible, Mark Dever

CHAPTER 1

Jesus' Discipleship Program

What do you think your pastor is doing right now? Maybe he is thinking of you, and praying for you and all the other members of your church. I would not be surprised if he is.

Maybe he is praying that you would grow in your relationship with Christ. Reading his Bible, he knows your relationship with Christ is connected to your love for other members of the church. He has studied verses like this one, where Jesus says,

> I give you a new command: Love one another. Just as I have loved you, you must also love one another. By this all people will know that you are My disciples, if you have love for one another. (John 13:34–35)

You should love your church like Jesus loved you, Christian. How did Jesus love you? By dying on the cross for the forgiveness of your sins, consecrating you to God. You cannot die for people's sin, of course, but you can help them remain consecrated to God. That's an old word, *consecrated*. But I find it useful. To consecrate something means to set it apart, to dedicate it to the Holy One. Christ has made the church holy. Your pastor, I trust, wants you to help them live out that holiness. And if you have God's Holy Spirit in you, you, too, want to help them be holy. To be a consecrated people.

At least, sometimes you feel this way, right?

The trouble is, pastors often try to help you and your fellow members take responsibility for one another by grabbing the latest discipleship-in-a-box program off the display table at their favorite pastors' conference. Inside that box or inside that best-selling book, they hear the story of some other pastor who grew a super huge church (God be praised!), where the lesson often is, "Here's what I did. You do it, too!" Maybe that will work for their churches. Maybe it won't.

I am not going to offer you a discipleship-in-a-box program. Instead, I want to point you to a discipleship-in-a-book program, the program that Jesus left in *his* book for both you and your pastor. This program is called—are you ready?—elder-led congregationalism.

A Change of Subject?

At this moment, I can hear a record player going "Scraaaaatch!" as if the needle got shoved off the spinning black disk. The room is suddenly silent. Everyone turns and stares. Then someone sneers, "Elder-led congregationalism?! To help with a church's discipling relationships?"

Yes, elder-led congregationalism.

"Are you serious?"

Yes, I'm serious.

"It's a mouth full."

I suppose it is.

"But isn't elder-led congregationalism, like, all about church government or something? It sounds like you just changed the subject."

No, I did not change the subject. Elder-led congregationalism is about church government, yes, but it is also the "program" that Jesus established to make the whole church responsible for the whole church, and to train every member for the work. It is Jesus' discipleship program.

Let me back up for a second. Typically, we think of the topic of church government as pertaining to who possesses the final authority in a church to make decisions. There are four basic positions:

- *Pastor or elder-led congregationalists* say the Bible gives this final authority to the gathered congregation as led by the pastors or elders. (I will use "pastors" and "elders" interchangeably throughout this book, as the New Testament does.)
- *Elder-rule* advocates say final authority belongs to the elders of an independent church.
- *Presbyterians* give authority to gatherings of elders over several churches.
- *Episcopalians* (Anglicans, Methodists, Roman Catholics, etc.) give a bishop authority over several churches.

People in all four positions acknowledge that Jesus and his Word possess *final* final authority. What divides these positions is who makes final decisions on matters like receiving members, church discipline, removing a disqualified elder, changing a statement of faith, approving a budget, and so forth.

On the whole, this book will not directly address these other models or try to defend elder-led congregationalism against their criticisms (but see the appendix!). This book is just too short for that. If you are interested in an apologetic work that dialogues with these other traditions, see my book *Don't Fire Your Church Members: The Case For Congregationalism* (B&H Academic, 2016). My goal here is just to ask what the Bible says.

That said, I have to admit that congregationalism hardly has a stellar reputation. Maybe you have heard the stories. On the sillier side, I think about the Baptist church who divided over the color of the shades in its sanctuary. Half the church wanted white and half wanted brown. So they hired a consultant who recommended . . . tan. (Hurray for the consultant!) On the more grieving side, you might have heard the news reports of the African-American couple who, a day before their wedding, received a phone call from their Baptist pastor. Would they mind if he married them down the street at the black church's building? Their predominantly white church was threatening to fire him if he performed their wedding in the church building. The pastor . . . submitted to the church. (Ugh!) In situations like these, congregationalism has been turned into a democracy. So churches vote on everything. Church business meetings feel like Town Hall debates. Pastors are treated like elected officials, to be thrown out of office if they don't give the voters what they want. (Yikes!)

And I'm calling this Jesus' discipleship program?

Such stories understandably sour people on congregationalism. After all, the Bible can hardly intend for whole churches to make decisions, much less divide over curtain colors, or to strong-arm their shepherds into discriminating against minorities, right?

Right. I don't want to call congregationalism a democracy, or to defend misuses of congregationalism. Fallen humans often misuse God's good gifts. Like the authority of parents and pastors, policemen and presidents, congregational authority is sometimes misused and misunderstood. There's no point in trying to sweep any of that dirt under the rug. But just because some marriages turn abusive does not mean we do away with marriage altogether, right?

Right. What we want is biblical congregationalism, and biblical congregationalism is *pastor* or *elder-led*. *Final* final authority, I said, belongs to Jesus and his Word. And the pastors speak for this Word. Where pastors lead, therefore, congregations should ordinarily follow. We will come back to the relationship between congregational authority and elder authority in chapter 5. For now, we can say that the church maintains final say on decisions concerning *what* they believe and *who* they are, or what I will unpack as the *what* and the *who* of the gospel in chapter 4; but the elders must lead the congregation through those very decisions.

This, I propose, is Jesus' discipleship program.

The Final Half of Jesus' Program: Congregational Responsibility

In order to understand what elder-led congregationalism has to do with discipleship, we need to think about its two halves. The *congregationalism* half requires you, the average church member, to take responsibility for other church members. It gives you this job.

In order to do your job, you must know the gospel. You must study the gospel. You must protect the gospel's ministry in your church. And you must work for the gospel's progress in the lives of your fellow church members and with outsiders. To put it another way, you must watch over your church, keeping it consecrated to God, just like Adam was to watch over the garden and Israel's priests were to watch over the temple, keeping them consecrated to God.

To be clear, I am assuming that possessing responsibility comes from possessing authority. A person is not responsible to do something they have not been authorized to do. Don't tell me I have a job if you won't give me the authority to do my job! That's like telling me to clean a building without giving me the keys to the building.

The fundamental claim of the congregationalism half, then, is that the gathered church possesses authority because Jesus expressly authorizes it and because he makes every gospel believer responsible for proclaiming and protecting his gospel and his gospel people, as later chapters will seek to demonstrate.

The Second Half of Jesus' Program: Elder Training

Yet think about this: who trains and equips gospel-believers to do their jobs? Who teaches them the gospel and how the gospel applies to every area of life? Who trains them to discern between true professions and false ones, so that they can keep the church consecrated to the Lord?

Pastors or elders!

That brings us to the *elder-led* half of Jesus' discipleship program. The congregation needs its leaders to train them in doing their jobs. Listen to how Paul puts it: Jesus "gave some to be . . . pastors and teachers, for the training of the saints in the work of ministry, to build up the body of Christ" (Eph. 4:11–12). What do pastors do? They train. What do the saints do? The work of the ministry. The two parts work together:

Elder-led → Gives you job training

Congregationalism → Gives you a job

This in a nutshell is Jesus' discipleship model. Or we can put it mathematically:

elder leadership **+** congregational rule **=** discipleship

Add these two variables and you have Jesus' program for discipleship.

People worry that congregationalism involves putting the church's decisions into the hands of its least mature members, as in the curtain-color and racist-church illustrations previously mentioned. It is true that if pastors do not train the saints, yes, the people will be immature and make bad decisions! But it is the very fact that elder-led congregationalism does not permit leaders simply to impose their will on the members, even the immature ones, that forces the leaders to do the work of training. Jesus' program requires the leaders to teach, explain, equip, shepherd, and woo their members toward maturity and the ability to make good decisions. The members are like sixteen-year-olds with car keys. You had better teach them to drive carefully, mom and dad! Don't blame the congregations for bad driving. Blame their teachers.

A church that gives all authority to its leaders hurts its own culture of discipling. Forsaking their own authority, the members become less responsible. They inch toward passivity and complacency and eventually worldliness. They leave the church less protected.

Meanwhile, the pastors who take away authority from their congregations, ironically, surrender one form of their own leadership by doing so. They are supposed to work hard at training the church to use its authority maturely. But if they relieve themselves of this responsibility, sure, their job will be easier, but they are not being the leaders that God intends.

Is biblical congregationalism a democracy? No, it is a mixed government—part monarchy (rule of the one), part oligarchy (rule of the few), part democracy (rule of the many). Jesus is King through his Word; the elders or pastors lead; and the congregation has final (human) say on certain crucial matters. And it is precisely the dynamic between the one, the few, and the many that cultivates a culture of discipleship, and that guides immature church members toward maturity.

Not Just the Church Business Meeting, But All of Life

Do you see? When Jesus and the apostles talked about church government, it wasn't just a discussion of bureaucratic decision-making. It was most fundamentally and importantly a matter of discipleship! Church government is about much more than what happens at what Baptists often call their church's business meeting.

Someone makes a motion. Someone else speaks against the motion. Eventually the church votes, maybe by voice, maybe by ballot.

Missing here is the bigger picture. What members do in those meetings should connect to what they do in their everyday lives by building relationships with one another. There should be a back-and-forth between making decisions and building relationships, like this:

making decisions → building relationships → making decisions → building...

Jesus intends for the people who make decisions to be the same people responsible for building relationships. Relationship building yields good decision making, because the decisions will be made with personal knowledge. And the responsibility to make decisions produces the incentive to build relationships, again, so that those decisions might be made with knowledge and therefore integrity.

Keeping the church consecrated to the Lord is an every day job. Was Adam supposed to keep his eyes peeled for lying serpents only on Sundays? Were the priests of Israel to separate "clean" from "unclean" in the temple only in a bi-monthly meeting? Of course not. The work of each was full-time: 24/7, as they say. And so is the church member's.

From the Gospel to a Gospel Order

The fact that church government is most fundamentally about discipleship also helps us to understand that not everything about church governance is situation-specific, but that our "gospel order" grows out of the gospel itself.

People sometimes say that the form of church government a church adopts should depend entirely upon a church's context. Your church might pick one form or another depending on the occasion, like you do with clothing. For the workday you can wear business casual, but for a wedding rehearsal you'll need a jacket and tie. Church government is that way too, right? Just make sure you have the right form for the occasion.

Certainly many things in a church's life will change between one time and place and another. But what I hope you discover in this book is that the trunk and branches of church government grow out of the seed of the gospel. The relationship between the gospel and our gospel-life together is not accidental. Rather, the gospel makes certain demands on the saints and our togetherness. The gospel produces a gospel order (by which I mean a church's governing structures), and that gospel order in turn displays and protects the gospel, like this:

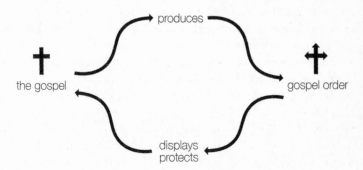

If you believe in the gospel, you will bind your life to other Christians. You will exercise a priestly care for the holiness of your fellow members. You will promote the gospel witness of your church in your community. And you will train to do this work by submitting your discipleship to fatherly guides, or shepherds. This isn't just the work of Sunday. This is a job that lasts all week.

Conclusion

Since the gospel's work has already begun in us, we are congregationalists. Since the gospel's work is not yet complete in us, we are elder-led congregationalists. Have you ever thought about the fact that there will be no pastors in heaven? Your pastor will have to find a new career since we'll all reign together with Christ (2 Tim. 2:12).

In the meantime, your pastor prays for you, teaches you, and sets an example for you. Not only that, he trains you to do your job. That's probably the most concise definition of elder-led congregationalism there is: your pastor training you to do your job. Or as Paul put it, elder-led congregationalism is Jesus giving you a pastor to train you for the work of ministry.

When practiced biblically, elder-led congregationalism is a gospel powerhouse. It . . .

- guards the gospel,
- matures the Christian disciple,
- strengthens the whole church,
- fortifies its holy integrity and witness,
- and equips the congregation to love their neighbors better in word and deed.

Do you want to grow in your discipleship to Christ, and protect the *who* and the *what* of the gospel? Then step into your congregational responsibilities as led by your pastors.

As I said a moment ago, my goal is not so much to persuade you of congregationalism, answering all the objections that might arise from a Presbyterian, Episcopalian, or an elder-rule perspective. Again, see *Don't Fire Your Church Members* if you need that. **The goal of this book is to help you understand from Scripture what your responsibilities are.** Jesus has assigned you with a job in the church, and you will grow in godliness as you undertake it. You might almost think of the book like your church job manual.

The road map here is pretty simple:

- Chapter 2 provides the big picture of what elder-led congregationalism looks like in the life of a church.
- Chapters 3 and 4 focus on the congregationalism half: your job.
- Chapter 5 focuses on the elder-led half: the elders' job training.
- The conclusion lists your job responsibilities.

The Big Picture

We could open our Bibles right now and begin, verse by verse, to build the biblical picture of elder-led congregationalism, Jesus' discipleship program. But that would be like asking you to put a 100-piece puzzle together without ever looking at the picture on the box. So in this chapter we will look at the picture on the box, and then in chapters 3 to 5 we will turn to the Scriptures in order to put the puzzle together.

Learning in Real Life

It was Sunday night. We were several minutes into a bimonthly meeting held just for members when an elder stood up to share this sad news with the church: "Dale has left his wife and children for another woman." The elder got choked up. Paused. Then went on: "A couple of the elders have been meeting with Dale for several months since the affair was discovered. At first he claimed to be sorry. But just recently he has moved out and has no plans of returning to his family." He explained how the wife was doing (not well), and what she thought of the elders' plans to tell the whole church (very grateful). He also discussed the kids (struggling).

The room was heavy. Seven hundred broken hearts heavy. It was like a sudden blow to the chest. You stagger backward. You regain your balance. You wait, uncertain of what to do next. But the chest throbs where the punch landed.

Then the elder did one more thing. He enlisted the whole room in the gospel work of pursuing this man, as well as in the gospel work of caring for this woman and her children. He said something like this: "Matthew 18 tells us that if a sinner does not listen to the two or three, tell it to the church. And if he doesn't listen to the church, treat him as you would an unbeliever. So we're telling you. If you have a relationship with Dale, please encourage him to repent and come back to his wife. If you don't have a relationship with Dale, please pray. If nothing changes between now and our next members' meeting in two months, the elders will return to you and recommend that we remove Dale from membership as an act of discipline." He also talked about a few ways to care for Dale's wife.

No formal action was taken by the congregation at this meeting. Members did ask a couple of questions, mostly about ways to serve the wife and children: "Do they need meals?" "Are there ways we can help with the kids' school?" "Should we say something when we see her?" But the main goal here was to inform and to enlist. The elders had been on the case for several months. The congregation's work would begin now: mostly in praying, for a few individuals in speaking to Dale, for a few other individuals in helping his wife and children, and eventually for the whole church in deciding to remove Dale from membership and the Lord's Table, if it came to that.

Now I want you to stop and reflect on this whole scenario, like you might study a photograph. What do you see?

I hope you see the two halves of Jesus' discipleship program: elder training and congregational responsibility.

Elder Training in Real Life

Think about what the elders presented to the congregation in that meeting. It was not a hypothetical sermon illustration. It was not a business school case study. It was not the effected reality of "reality television." No. It was a real, live family crisis in the church. It was as real and present and tangible as mom sitting down at the dinner table with the kids and saying, "Daddy has left." Now the elders were asking the congregation to sit down at that table with that family. To be there. To comfort the children. To weep with the wife. To admonish the abandoner. To mentally and emotionally process the whole situation for themselves, and to manage their way through it together. Not for pretend, but for real.

The elders followed Jesus' instruction to "tell the church" (Matt. 18:17), and then they trained the congregation to respond according to the gospel. Their leadership taught the church at least five lessons.

First, we are saved by grace alone through faith alone. Were that not the case, Dale would have ceased being a Christian immediately, and there would have been no point in pursuing him for repentance. Removal would have been automatic. But praise God that isn't the case.

Second, we are saved by faith alone, but the faith that saves is never alone. So this man, when confronted—would he repent? After all, Christians eventually repent when confronted in their sin. The Holy Spirit gives them godly sorrow instead of worldly sorrow. (Paul explains both kinds in 2 Corinthians 7:9–11.) They will cut off their hand or gouge out their eye rather than continue in sin.

Third, the gospel saves not just individuals, but a body. God has "put the body together" such that "if one member suffers, all the members suffer with it" (1 Cor. 12:24, 26). This man and this wife were *part of our own body*. We all shared in the grief and suffering. And now we all were responsible to act.

Fourth, the elders' leadership taught the congregation what gospel love looks like. It does not look like live-and-let-live. It is not divorced from truth, holiness, and obedience. Nor does gospel love look like self-righteous finger-pointing or angry, furrowed brows. Rather, gospel love looks like forgiven sinners warning against the way of death and pointing to the way of life. It speaks truthfully, sometimes with tears, always with prayer and compassion.

To be sure, the elders might have been tempted to hide all this difficult adultery business behind elder meeting-room doors. That would have been cleaner, more efficient, less risky. Besides, all of these gospel lessons could be taught through sermons, right?

Perhaps. But there is a difference between asking a teenager to read a car owner's manual and putting the keys in her hand and saying, "Here, you drive. But follow my instructions carefully." Stories about sin and its consequences can be helpful, but walking a church through it puts those lessons into 3D.

So fast-forward two months. The next members' meeting came. Nothing had changed in Dale's life. He resisted all the church's efforts to call him to repentance. So the church voted to remove him from membership and the Lord's Table. We excommunicated him, to use some older language. This means we were no longer willing to affirm him publicly as a Christian.

This brings us to a fifth lesson that the whole exercise taught the church: what it means to act with gospel courage. Saying "yes" to removing someone from membership can be scary. It makes you swallow hard. Put yourself in the mind of a sixteen-year-old who has never driven: *This is not just reading an owner's manual. This is putting the car in drive and stepping on the gas. Will it hit something?*

By obeying Jesus' command to "tell it to the church," the elders discipled the congregation through all five of these lessons and probably more. And each of these lessons would transmit to the rest of life. Maybe another wife in the church is dealing with her husband who claims to love Jesus but demonstrates a pattern of deceit. Maybe a friend with whom you've been sharing the gospel claims to have become a Christian but won't join a church or stop getting drunk. Maybe you call yourself a Christian, but you are living in unrepentant sin of some form. The few lessons the church learned in this situation come into play in all sorts of ways. We learn the importance of discerning between godly sorrow and worldly sorrow. We learn the courage of speaking honestly and drawing lines with tenderness and tears.

Working through gospel-life issues corporately trains us in handling them individually. When these meetings occur behind closed elder-meeting or bishop doors, such training does not occur.

Elder-led congregationalism, in short, requires the elders to teach and to disciple, both for the good of those directly involved but also for the good of the whole congregation.

What Is Excommunication?

Roman Catholicism has used the word *excommunication* to describe the process of removing people from church membership *and* salvation—as if the church could deny salvation. Among Protestants, excommunication simply means removing members from membership in the church and the Lord's Table (a person is ex-communion-ed). It is a church's way of saying, "We can no longer lend our corporate kingdom name to affirming that this individual is a Christian."

Congregational Responsibility

Of course, the foundation of this whole discipleship process was the fact that every member jointly owned final responsibility for whether we would continue to affirm Dale's profession of faith. That is the second thing to notice in this snapshot of Jesus' discipleship program: congregational responsibility. The elders led the process by making their recommendations at each step. But the church still had a decision to make and an action to take.

A similar dynamic shows up in 1 Corinthians 5 between the apostle Paul and the Corinthian church, where Paul challenges them about an adulterer in their midst. Paul says of the adulterer, "I have already pronounced judgment on the one who did such a thing" (1 Cor. 5:3 ESV). Then he calls upon the church to exercise judgment for themselves: "Is it not those inside the church whom you are to *judge*?" (v. 12, italics added). The noun in verse 3 ("judgment") assumes a verbal form in verse 12 ("to judge"). What Paul did, the church was to do. They bore final responsibility. After all, he would not always be there to help them with their decisions.

So it was in my church. We elders had pronounced a judgment among ourselves concerning Dale in our Thursday night elders meetings. Then we turned to the congregation and asked them to exercise the same judgment for themselves in our Sunday night members meetings. We placed the decision back into their hands because we understood from Scripture that responsibility finally belonged to them.

Making Decisions and Building Relationships: A Virtuous Cycle

Focusing just on a two-hour meeting, however, might cause you to miss the bigger picture. The church's responsibility to act in the meeting is part and parcel of their larger responsibility to care for one another throughout the week. The fact is, if you only focus on the meeting, you're just glancing at a photograph. What we really need is a video camera that records the members' lives together before and after the meetings.

Recall what I said in the last chapter about the relationship between making decisions in a meeting and building relationships outside of it. There is a virtuous cycle between these two activities. Each benefits the other.

As it turns out, Dale made himself inaccessible to the church outside of our members meetings. He did not want to hear from anyone. Dale's wife and children, however, were quickly absorbed by the congregation: helping with meals, housing, tutoring for the kids, finances, and more. All of this "life together" stuff outside of the meeting gave integrity, meaningfulness, and honesty to the decisions required of the church inside the meeting. The church could have just taken the elders' word for what Dale did. But they didn't have to. They babysat Dale's kids in order for Dale's wife, now effectively a single mom, to run her errands. They experienced the pain on her face and the exhaustion in her shoulders.

But it is not just what happens outside the meeting that enriches and gives credibility to what we do in the meeting. The meetings help us understand our shared responsibility for Dale, his wife, and his children outside the meeting. The meetings confer responsibility and commission us in the program of care and discipleship. "Oh, yes, I'm responsible for them. I had better act."

Congregationalism Versus Non-Congregationalism

Now, I have used an illustration for elder-led congregationalism involving excommunication. But there is much more to a congregation's work, most of it joy-giving, like choosing elders or receiving members. The essence of congregational authority revolves around what we believe and who we are, or what I will characterize in chapter 4 as the *what* and the *who* of the gospel. Every member must know the gospel well enough to protect it. Every member must know other members well enough to help them remain faithful to the gospel. Every member must work to help a church remain faithful from one generation to the next, consecrated to the Lord. Recall what I said in the last chapter: the gospel produces a gospel order, and that gospel order in turn displays and protects the gospel. Elder-led congregationalism is fundamentally about living out and guarding the gospel.

Consider a non-congregational church by comparison. Only a small group of individuals possess final responsibility for the church's gospel ministry and faithfulness. They alone must know the members of the church well enough to discern hypocrites and heretics. They alone must protect right doctrine. They alone are finally accountable for preserving the church. The difference is profound.

You might compare a congregational and non-congregational model of church government to two different exercise classes, one in which the trainer does the workout while the whole class watches, and another in which the trainer demonstrates the exercises and then tells everyone to get to work. Which class will be healthier? Or consider two different construction crews, one where only the foreman works, and another where the whole crew works. Which crew will build more houses?

In elder-led congregationalism, the weekly gathering is for job training. It is where the pastors equip the members to know the gospel, to live by the gospel, to protect the church's gospel witness, and to extend the gospel's reach into one another's lives and among outsiders. The pastors equip the saints to build up the church, says Paul (Eph. 4:11–13). Who builds up the church? The members.

What this means, furthermore, is that church government never gets left behind in the Christian's life. We don't leave it on the church building steps on the way out the door. All week long every church member works to promote and protect the church. All week you work to separate the holy from the unholy, both in your life and in the lives of your fellow church members.

Elder-led congregationalism offers us Jesus' *daily* discipleship program. It trains and strengthens Christians, teaches them to recognize the counterfeits, protects the church's gospel witness, encourages fellowship, guards against complacency and nominalism, and equips the saints for fulfilling the church's mission.

The Bottom Line: You Have a Job to Do

So there it is—the picture of the puzzle on the box all put together. That is elder-led congregationalism. And the big picture illustrates this: you and your elders both have jobs to do. Together with the other members of your church, *you* are finally responsible for the church's gospel faithfulness. *Your elders* are responsible to train you to carry out that job.

Now, to look at the pieces one by one, we turn to the Scriptures.

CHAPTER 3

Adam Had a Job

If I had 40 seconds with you on an elevator, and you asked me where congregationalism is in the Bible, I would say something like this:

> Well, in Matthew 18:15–20, Jesus gives the local church final authority in a case of church discipline. Paul does the same in 1 Corinthians 5. He does not tell the leaders to remove the unrepentant adulterer from the church. He tells the church to do it. Then in Galatians 1:6–9, Paul treats the Galatian churches as capable of removing even him—an apostle!—if he teaches a wrong gospel. And in 2 Corinthians 2:6, Paul refers to a case of church discipline having been decided by a "majority." And all of this, I would say, argues that the gathered congregation possesses final authority over the *who* and the *what* of the gospel.

I assume I could say that on an elevator, at least if the ride was longer than a couple of floors.

But suppose you knew something about Presbyterian or Anglican polity. You just might step off the elevator, turn back toward me, and say in the time it takes the elevator door to close, "But what about Hebrews 13:17: 'Obey your leaders and submit to them'?"

The conversation, now concluded courtesy of an elevator door, leaves us in the one of two places where most people who have thought about the topic for more then 40 seconds place themselves:

either looking to the group of Bible verses that give authority to the congregation, or looking at the group of verses that give authority to the leaders. The temptation always is to pick your favorite group of verses and ignore the other group. And everyone has their favorites. The Roman Catholics love Matthew 16. The Baptists, Matthew 18 and 1 Corinthians 5. Anglicans and Presbyterians, Acts 15 and Hebrews 13.

Ultimately, we need both groups of verses for Jesus' discipleship program, because that gives us the two halves of elder-led congregationalism. But understanding what the Bible says about church government takes more than a 40-second elevator ride and reciting our favorite proof-texts. As surprising as it may sound, we need to trace a story line that runs through the whole Bible, a story that is especially important for understanding the congregational half of elder-led congregationalism. In fact, it's that story line which provides the church member with his or her job title: *priest-king*.

Does that sound like a strange title? It is the job or office that God first gave to Adam in Genesis 1 and 2. Then it was passed along to Abraham, then Israel, then David, and was then fulfilled in the person and work of Jesus Christ, to whom the church is united.

We'll unpack this in more detail through the next two chapters, but suffice it to say for now that to make a person a church member is to reinstall that person into the office of priest-king that began with Adam. As priest-king in Eden, Adam was supposed to "work" and to "watch over" the garden in which God had placed him (Gen. 2:15). He was to keep the place where God dwelled consecrated to God, cultivating it and protecting it from evil. So it is today with every church member. He or she, too, is called to work and watch over the dwelling place of God, the church, keeping it consecrated to God. I will explain the office of priest-king in this chapter and then connect it to church membership more clearly in the next.

So what is a priest-king?

The Story of the Priest-King: Adam

The whole-Bible story starts with God's covenant with Adam. God created Adam and immediately installed him as a king over the rest of creation. He said to Adam, "Be fruitful, multiply, fill the earth, and subdue it. Rule the fish of the sea, the birds of the sky, and every creature that crawls on the earth" (Gen. 1:28). Adam, this first king, was supposed to push back the borders of Eden, to fill the land with children, to subdue new territory, and to rule over everything.

In Genesis 2, God tells Adam to "work" and "watch over" the garden of Eden (v. 15). Remarkably, this was the very same job description God would eventually give Israel's priests—that is, to "work" and "watch over" the tabernacle/temple, keeping it consecrated to the Lord (Num. 3:7–8; 8:26; 18:5–6). To that end, priests were charged with naming things as "clean" or "unclean," and "holy" or "unholy." God specially dwelled in the temple, and therefore the priest's work was to maintain the temple as a holy place. Adam's work was the same as the priests'—maintain and protect the garden as a holy place, as the dwelling place of God himself.

What Is a Priest-King?

If a king rules, a priest-king rules on behalf of a greater king, God. That is, the priest-king *mediates* God's rule and works to protect what's holy.

Now ordinarily we think of kings as sitting at the top of the totem pole. But notice that King Adam was under God. He was, in other words, a *mediating* king, and so he was—you might say—a *priest-king*, tasked with mediating between God and creation. (That's what a priest does—he *mediates* or stands between God and his creatures.) In the beginning, God's temple was not a particular building. It was the garden. Since God dwelled there, Adam was responsible to keep the holy separated from the unholy, consecrated to the Lord. And he was to do this by protecting the garden: "Watch out for lying serpents, Adam. And be sure to pass along my commands to your wife as well."

Besides being a real historical person, it's important to realize that Adam was also *Everyman*, representing all of us. Psalm 8 teaches that God has made every human being a king like Adam. God has "crowned" and made every human "lord" over the work of God's hands (Ps. 8:4–8). Humanity, remarkably, is a democracy of kings!

Abraham, Moses, David, and a New Covenant

Sadly, Adam did not live as the perfect priest-king. He did not represent God's rule but sought his own rule. So God fired Adam, evicting him from the garden.

Abraham

He then offered the job to Abraham. Only this time, God didn't just command, "Be fruitful." Instead, he promised, "I will make you extremely fruitful and will make nations and kings come from you" (Gen. 17:6).

God himself fulfilled in Abraham what he commanded of Adam. Abraham would be this mediating king, or priest-king. The nations would be blessed through him as he taught his children "to keep the way of the LORD by doing what is right and just" (Gen. 18:18–19).

Moses

God more fully explained "the way of the LORD" through the covenant with Moses and the people of Israel. Right before he gave Moses and Israel this covenant, God said, "If you will listen to Me and carefully keep My covenant, you will be My own possession out of all the peoples" and "My kingdom of priests and My holy nation" (Exod. 19:5–6). What was an *individual* office became a *corporate* office.

The whole nation now would occupy the office of priest-king. Together they would demonstrate what holiness looks like by being a people consecrated to the Lord.

Interestingly, the Mosaic Covenant also separated out a class of citizens known as priests. The purpose of this office was to highlight the lesson of what it means to be holy or consecrated to the Lord.

David

God also separated out the office of king through the covenant with David (see 2 Sam. 7; Pss. 2; 110), and commanded the king to write out a copy of his law, to read it all the days of his life, to fear the Lord, and to obey it (Deut. 17:18–19). David's job was not to be a priest, but his rule was to be priestly.

Tragically, the story of Israel and its kings might be titled "The Fall—Part Two." Only now the drama stretched out over a millennium and was set on an international stage. The lesson was plain: we cannot save ourselves or walk in righteousness. We need God himself to fix our guilt problem and our obedience problem.

A New Covenant

So God promised a new covenant, one by which God would make provision for the forgiveness of sins and enable the people to obey by placing his law on their hearts (Isa. 53—54; Jer. 31:31–34; Ezek. 36:24–27). The dwelling place of God's people would again become "like the garden of Eden" (Ezek. 36:35).

Furthermore, God's people would no longer be dependent on the offices of temple priest or Davidic king in order to know God. "No longer will one teach his neighbor or his brother, saying, 'Know the Lord,' for they will all know Me, from the least to the greatest of them" (Jer. 31:34). These two offices would collapse back upon every covenant member. Everyone would have direct and equal access to God and to the knowledge of him. The office of priest-king would be fully democratized once more.

Jesus and the Church

Jesus

The Bible has lots of names for Jesus based on the work he came to do. Among them he is characterized as the new Adam, the seed of Abraham, the new Israel, and David's greater son. Why? Because he, finally, did the job they were supposed to do but failed to do. He was the perfect priest and perfect king in his life, death, and resurrection.

Jesus rules on God's behalf as the firstborn of a new creation. He visibly reestablished God's kingdom in his own person. And like Adam, he was a Representative or Everyman. But this Representative didn't bring death, he brought life. He offered a new covenant in his blood, a sacrifice of atonement whereby we were not only forgiven of sin but actually *united* to him so that what he is, we are.

This is the glory of the gospel. We rise because he is risen. We are declared righteous because he was declared righteous. And—here's the kicker—we reign because he reigns!

Do you see? When you become united to Christ by faith, the same office which he holds falls also to you. You become, because of your union with him, a priest-king once again. That's why Peter can say, "You are a chosen race, a royal priesthood, a holy nation, a people for His possession" (1 Pet. 2:9). Just think about those four labels. Christians are . . .

- a new creation race (new Adams),
- a democracy of ruling priests (like Adam),
- a set apart nation (a new Israel),
- and a people for God.

The church occupies this office corporately, like Israel did. But also, every member of the church occupies this office individually, like Adam. There is no separate class of priests or kings. Every member of your church is both: Jim, Sue, Fred, Barney, Farhod, Enoch, Isabella, Zoe . . . all priest-kings, by virtue of their union with Christ.

The Responsibility of a Priest-King

This story of the priest-king in the Bible beginning with Adam is crucial as we think about who possesses authority in the church.

Let's start with the responsibilities of a priest-king. How was Adam supposed to fulfill his *kingly* duties? By working, cultivating, and pushing out the boundaries of the garden. How was he to fulfill his *priestly* duties? By watching over the garden and keeping it consecrated to the Lord and the Lord's purposes.

Christians, the priest-kings of the New Testament, must work and watch over something, too. What? The church, the temple of the New Testament (1 Cor. 3:16; cf. 6:19; 1 Pet. 2:4–8). God specially dwells there, among them, just like he dwelled in Adam's garden and Israel's temple: "For where two or three are gathered together in My name, I am there among them" (Matt. 18:20). Therefore every member of Christ's universal church is responsible to keep the holy separated from the unholy in the church. And Christians must do that in the very place where the universal church becomes visible—the local church. These church members, furthermore, are responsible to be fruitful and multiply and rule like kings. How? By going, making disciples, baptizing, and teaching (Matt. 28:19–20). Everyman Adam's job becomes every Christian and church member's job.

Encouraging the Corinthians in their priestly protective work, Paul charges the members of the Corinthian church to consider carefully with whom they partner. Notice how he talks to them as if they were Old Testament priests responsible for keeping the holy and the unholy separate:

> Do not be mismatched with unbelievers. For what partnership
> is there between righteousness and lawlessness? . . . Or what

> does a believer have in common with an unbeliever? . . . For
> we are the sanctuary of the living God, as God said: I will dwell
> among them and walk among them, and I will be their God,
> and they will be My people. Therefore, come out from among
> them and be separate, says the Lord; do not touch any unclean
> thing, and I will welcome you. (2 Cor. 6:14–17)

Paul is not talking about keeping the temple censers and pans ceremonially clean. He is talking about remaining separate from people who profess to be Christians but whose false teaching or living indicates otherwise. Paul intends every single Christian, as part of his or her priestly duties, to keep watch over who belongs to the church and who doesn't.

And this priestly work of watching over the church goes hand in hand with the kingly work of expanding and multiplying. Paul, just a few verses earlier, affirmed that he and the Corinthians were "ambassadors for Christ" who possessed a "ministry of reconciliation" (5:18, 20). Through evangelism, the members of the Corinthian church were to do what they could to push back the boundaries of the church—like Adam in the garden—subduing the territory of human hearts on behalf of the great King.

The Ability of a Priest-King

Yet the New Testament treats believers as not only responsible for doing the work of a priest-king, but *able* to do it.

Think again of Jeremiah's promise of a democratized priestly rule: "No longer will one teach his neighbor or his brother, saying, 'Know the Lord,' for they will all know Me, from the least to the greatest." This is the lesson that Jesus and the apostles apply to the church. Jesus tells his disciples to not be called "Rabbi" because there is only one Teacher (Matt. 23:8). Paul says the church has not been taught by human wisdom but by the Spirit (1 Cor. 2:10–16). John says that the saints have been anointed and don't need a teacher (1 John 2:20, 27; see also Matt. 23:8).

In short, the New Testament affirms that the Holy Spirit indwells every believer, enabling him or her to separate the true gospel from a false gospel, or a true knowledge of God from a false knowledge. They are responsible to be Christ's priest-kings, and they are able.

One implication is that Christians are also responsible and able to affirm *what* counts as true doctrine. The apostle John therefore tells his readers (ordinary Christians) to "test the spirits," which they do by determining if a spirit "confesses that Jesus Christ has come in the flesh" (1 John 4:1–2). Peter wants to "develop a genuine understanding" among his readers (ordinary Christians) so that they can keep "guard" between false teaching and true (2 Pet. 3:1–2, 17–18). And Paul admonishes his readers (ordinary Christians) for listening to a wrong gospel in their churches (Gal. 1:6–9). The saints don't need a seminary degree to discern between good teaching and bad. They don't need to be ordained. The Spirit of God and Scripture provide all the training they need.

A second implication is that Christians are both responsible and able to affirm *who* belongs to the gospel and to God. They should be able to assess one another's professions of faith. That implication is explicit in our elevator texts of Matthew 18 and 1 Corinthians 5, which we will explore further in the next chapter.

Conclusion

I'm sure you've noticed by now that I haven't unpacked the most important New Testament texts for congregationalism. Yes, I mentioned them briefly on our elevator ride, but we haven't taken the time to consider them carefully, much less have we considered how they relate to other verses that affirm pastor or elder leadership.

Instead, I have tried to show you that far, far more is going on here than elevator-ride proof texts can possibly convey. Something grand is unfolding in the story line of the Bible, a story more epic than a *Lord of the Rings* trilogy or *Star Wars* saga. God deputized Adam as a priest-king. Yet Adam rebelled and was exiled. The royal scepter and priestly miter then passed on to Abraham, Israel, David, and finally the beloved Son, the last Everyman. Jesus, this head of God's new covenant people, fulfilled the office of priest-king perfectly, both for his own sake and on behalf of his people.

But then even more amazingly, these people—you and me, if we're Christians!—have now been hired and deputized through Christ to fulfill Adam's original office. This involves representing Christ, seeking to expand the reach of Christ's kingdom and guarding the people of God in holiness, which means watching over both the *what* of the knowledge of God and the *who* of God's people. Every Christian has this job assignment. A pastor, presbytery, or bishop that prevents church members from doing this work, therefore, essentially *fires* them from the work God in Christ has charged them to do.

At least the Bible's story line would seem to say as much. What else does the New Testament say?

CHAPTER 4

Now Jesus Gives the Job to Your Church

In the last chapter, I argued that becoming a Christian means being reinstalled in Adam's office of priest-king. But exactly how do you carry out this job assignment? You may be hired by Jesus, but how do you actually show up for work? Answer: you get baptized and join a church. Church membership is what makes your priest-king job assignment public and practical.

> Church membership makes your priest-king job assignment public and practical.

Protestants love to talk about the Great Commission in Matthew 28. But there are two other chapters in Matthew that they don't talk so much about, yet are crucial for rightly understanding the work of the church. Those are Matthew 16 and 18, where Jesus teaches about something called "the keys of the kingdom." The thing is, Matthew 16 and 18 are the only places that Jesus ever uses the word *church*, which tells me we should pay closer attention to those chapters than we usually do. Not only so, but those two chapters are actually crucial for understanding Matthew 28 rightly because the same themes surface in chapters 16, 18, and 28. Fair warning before we dive in: This chapter will offer the most painstaking, brick-by-brick explanation in this book. So prepare to walk slowly. But it's also probably the most important chapter. So don't skip it!

The four questions this chapter attempts to answer are:

- What authority does Jesus give to a congregation?
- What exactly is a church?
- How does the church exercise its authority?
- When does the church exercise its authority?

By answering those questions, we will get a better grip on the nature of your job and how you show up for work.

What Authority Does Jesus Give to a Congregation?

What authority does Jesus give to individual churches? Answer: he gives them the keys of the kingdom.

In Matthew 16:13 Jesus asks his disciples, "Who do people say that the Son of Man is?" And again in verse 15: "Who do you say that I am?" He asks "who" twice, but he appears interested both in a *what* and a *who*: What is a right confession? And who of you knows it?

Simon Peter answers, "You are the Messiah, the Son of the living God" (v. 16). Jesus affirms Peter's answer on behalf of "My Father in heaven" (v. 17). And then Jesus observes,

> "And I also say to you that you are Peter, and on this rock I
> will build My church, and the forces of Hades will not over-
> power it. I will give you the keys of the kingdom of heaven,
> and whatever you bind on earth is already bound in heaven,
> and whatever you loose on earth is already loosed in heaven."
> (Matt. 16:18–19)

Notice what Jesus does here. First, he promises that he's going to build his church on this rock—this confessor confessing the right confession. Second, in order to build this church, Jesus gives Peter, who represents the apostles, the keys of the kingdom for binding and loosing.

But Peter and the apostles are not the only people to receive the keys. If we jump to Matthew 18, we see that Jesus also gives the keys to a gathered assembly—a local church. The context is a scenario of church discipline in which a "brother," or Christian, is caught in sin:

> "If your brother sins against you, go and rebuke him in private.
> If he listens to you, you have won your brother. But if he won't
> listen, take one or two more with you, so that by the testimony
> of two or three witnesses every fact may be established. If he
> pays no attention to them, tell the church. But if he doesn't pay
> attention even to the church, let him be like an unbeliever and
> a tax collector to you." (vv. 15–17)

The scenario envisions three rounds of evaluation and judgment over a person's sin. First, an individual must confront, evaluate, and render judgment. Then two or three must repeat the process. Then the whole church must evaluate and render judgment. Jesus does not conclude the process with the church leaders. He progresses from one, to a few, to an assembly, which is a literal translation of the word *church*. And *assembly* means assembly. Letting a subgroup of the church (like the leaders) remove a member not only interrupts Jesus' numeric progression, it divides the church. Some would know the person is out, some would not. That's not the picture Jesus paints here. Rather, the whole congregation is the final court of appeal for evaluation and judgment.

Verses 18 affirms that fact: "I assure you: Whatever you bind on earth is already bound in heaven, and whatever you loose on earth is already loosed in heaven." Sound familiar? That's because it's the language Jesus used when talking about the keys with Peter. Only this time, he is not talking to just one person. The "you" in verse 18 is plural. In Texas, they might say, "Whatever y'all bind on earth . . . whatever y'all loose on earth . . . ." The point is, he is giving the keys of the kingdom to the gathered church. The gathered church has the authority to remove someone from membership (v. 17) because it possesses the keys of binding and loosing (v. 18).

All this might seem a bit complicated. But look at the title of this book again: *Understanding the Congregation's Authority*. Right now we are at the burning-hot center of understanding the church's authority. The gathered church has authority because Jesus gave it the keys of the kingdom. Not the pope. Not the elders. Not a general assembly. None of these characters show up in Matthew 18, and nowhere else in the New Testament are such groups connected to the keys.

Still, we are left with the $64,000 question, what does it mean to say that churches possess the authority of the keys to bind or loose? As I have argued at length in a number of other works, it means that churches can exercise the same authority that Jesus exercised with Peter in chapter 16, or that the local church exercises in chapter 18: the authority to stand in front of a gospel confessor, to consider his or her gospel confession and life, and to announce an official judgment on heaven's behalf: "That is/isn't a right gospel confession" and "That is/isn't a true gospel confessor." Exercising the keys is rendering judgment on a *gospel what* and a *gospel who*, a confession and a confessor.

The work is very much comparable to the work that a courtroom judge does. A judge doesn't make the law; and he doesn't make a person innocent or guilty. He interprets the law; he "interprets" the person; and then he pronounces judgment. He pounds the gavel and pronounces "Guilty" or "Not guilty."

What Is the Authority of the Keys?

It is the authority to pronounce heaven's judgment on the *what* and *who* of the gospel—confessions and confessors. More concretely, it is the authority to write and affirm statements of faith and to add or remove names in the church membership directory.

So it is with key-wielding churches. They don't make the gospel what it is. They don't make a person a Christian or not. Rather, they listen to what a Christian is confessing; they consider the confessor's life, and they render a judgment on heaven's behalf. They make a public pronouncement with the "Bam!" of a gavel: "Member of the church" or "Not a member."

That pronouncement doesn't merely *teach*, like a law professor who teaches about the law in his classroom. That pronouncement *binds* (or *looses*). Like glue. Like rope. Like a judge's pronouncement of innocence or guilt. And when a judge pronounces, his verdict unleashes a series of legal consequences and/or benefits.

The same thing happens when churches speak on behalf of Christ. Their pronouncements have real effects, consequences, and benefits. They either bring a person into membership or separate a person out of it.

To put it another way, the keys make membership in the new covenant and citizenship in Christ's kingdom "visible." Think about it: the nation of Israel could be publicly identified among the peoples of the earth by circumcision, Sabbath-keeping, and eventually a land. Israel was visible. But membership in the Spirit-given, Christ-won new covenant and kingdom is invisible. How do you make membership visible? How does it "go public" so that the peoples of the earth know who belongs and who doesn't? And how do we Christians know who "we" are? Answer: gatherings of Christians employ the keys of the kingdom for binding and loosing.

In the most down-to-earth terms, the keys allow local churches to write and affirm statements of faith, which define the gospel. And they allow churches to add or remove names in their membership directories, which define who the people of God are.

Isn't this stunning? Jesus did not go to the wise, powerful, or noble ones to represent his authority on Planet Earth. He did not ask the kings, philosophers, or poets, the Ivy League college or the college of cardinals, to represent his rule. Instead, he went to the foolish, weak, insignificant, and despised (1 Cor. 1:26–28). He went to ordinary Christian folk and church members and gave them the keys of the kingdom of heaven. He said, "You speak for me. You make a royal and priestly judgment for the Father in heaven. Tell the nations, 'That is a right confession!' and 'He/she is a true confessor!'"

What authority does Christ give to the gathered congregation? He gives it the authority of the keys.

Where Are the Keys Exercised?

Having said all that, it can feel like the church sort of just shows up in these verses. What exactly is a church? Does Jesus define it anywhere?

In fact he does—in Matthew 18:20: "For where two or three are gathered together in My name, I am there among them." I unpack this whole passage and verse in greater depth in *Don't Fire Your Church Members*, but let me briefly say here, this verse is not about praying with a small group in your church. This verse is all about authority.

I will admit, verse 20 confounded me for some time. Why does Jesus say two or three? Who are they? Well, you need at least two people to be a church. Less than two is not an assembly.

What Is Church Membership?

A covenant between believers whereby they affirm one another's professions of faith through the ordinances and agree to oversee one another's discipleship to Christ.

More importantly, Jesus is invoking the principle he already mentioned in verse 16: that ancient Jewish law about two or three witnesses. In Deuteronomy 19, God says that two or three witnesses must agree for a formal charge in a Jewish court to be binding. That law created a powerful testimony to the truth because it involved those two or three witnesses in bearing testimony not only to the truth of the matter, but also to the truth of each other's testimony *about* the truth of the matter! But now Jesus takes that old law and applies it to a new situation. These two or three gather to testify to Jesus' name: "where two or three are gathered in My name." But by testifying to Jesus' name, they have to testify to their agreement with each other. Like this:

Person 1: "Hey, you just said you believed in Jesus. I do too!"

Person 2: "That's great. But wait a second. Are we talking about the same Jesus? I mean, I'm not talking about the Mormon Jesus or the Jehovah's Witness Jesus or the he's-just-a-great-teacher Jesus. I'm talking about the fully God, fully man, died on the cross for sins and rose again Jesus."

Person 1: "That's exactly who I'm talking about!"

Person 2: "Great, let's regularly gather in his name to proclaim it."

Person 1: "You got it!"

Person 3: "Hey guys, I've been listening to you talk. Can I join you? This is the same Jesus who redeemed me too."

Persons 1 and 2: "Wonderful!"

Notice that in this situation, you have two or three people willing to testify to who Jesus is, testify to one another's professions of faith, and do all of this as they regularly gather together. Here, in this gathering, this ancient Jewish law applies and holds confessors together like some sort of glue. It *binds* them, like a covenant binds.

Jesus then seals the covenant by saying he is "there among them." That doesn't mean he hovers in the room like some mystical fog. No, it means he identifies his person and authority with those people, just like God did with the people of Israel through the temple. He means they can fly his flag. The context, remember, is exercising the keys and speaking on behalf of heaven. These two or three become . . . drumroll, please . . . a church! And as a church, they are licensed to exercise the keys and officially speak on heaven's behalf.

So when you and a number of other Christians—Jim, Sue, Fred, Barney, Farhod, Enoch, Isabella, Zoe, or whatever their names are—have that conversation I just described, and then you agree to regularly gather to proclaim Jesus' name, Jesus promises to place his name and authority upon your gathering and count you as a church! You can raise his flag. And each of you are now its members.

Amazing, right?

The basic unit of kingdom authority on earth is not at the Vatican. It's not at denominational headquarters. It's not your Thursday night elders meeting. It's your gathered church. Also, it is not something smaller, like a small group. Again, that would mean division in the church, each small group claiming to speak for Jesus relative to other small groups. And Jesus didn't make the late-twentieth-century "small group" his basic unit of kingdom authority. Kingdom authority—the authority of the keys—is tied to the gathered church.

So what exactly is a church? I will answer that a little more elegantly after discussing the ordinances (next section), but just to provide a slightly more technical engineer's definition—think of this as the blueprints—we can say that a church is a group of Christians who, with the authority of Christ's keys, covenant together as Christ followers and fellow citizens of his kingdom by gathering together to proclaim his name.

How Does the Church Exercise Its Authority?

All right, how then does a church exercise the authority of the keys, exactly? Answer: through baptism and the Lord's Supper. Consider the Great Commission in Matthew 28.

> Then Jesus came near and said to them, "All authority has been given to Me in heaven and on earth. Go, therefore, and make disciples of all nations, baptizing them in the name of the Father and of the Son and of the Holy Spirit, teaching them to

observe everything I have commanded you. And remember, I
am with you always, to the end of the age." (vv. 18–20)

Three things are worth observing here:

First, making a disciple requires us to baptize and teach.

Second, baptism publicly identifies someone with God. A person
is baptized "into the name" of the Father, the Son, and the Spirit. It
gives a person a nametag with Jesus' name on it.

Third, Jesus, once again, ties his presence to these disciple-makers
who baptize and teach: "And behold, I am with you always, to the end
of the age."

Putting these observations together, I think it becomes clear that
we should read Matthew 28 not in isolation, as Christians often do, but
with Matthew 16 and 18 in mind. The people who gather in Christ's
name with keys in hand, presumably, possess the authority to baptize
in Christ's name. And the people with whom he dwells now, presumably, are the people with whom he will dwell always. If Matthew 16
and 18 authorize churches to represent heaven, Matthew 28 shows how
they get to work. This means, crucially, that the Great Commission is
given to churches, not just to individual Christians.

> Churches, not just individual Christians, fulfill the
> Great Commission.

A second implication follows: a church member's job responsibilities include not just exercising the keys, but fulfilling the Great
Commission by making disciples. To be sure, sharing the gospel,
affirming the gospel, admitting people into membership, and protecting the church from hypocrites and heretics all work together. They are
mutually reinforcing, and part of making disciples.

Finally, think about the Lord's Supper, the new covenant, and the
church. The Supper is a sign of the covenant. "For this is My blood

that establishes the covenant," says Jesus (Matt. 26:28). Also, the Supper reveals a church as a church. "Because there is one bread," Paul says, "we who are many are one body, for all of us share that one bread" (1 Cor. 10:17; 11:29). We should not be surprised then that Paul reserves the Supper for church gatherings: "when you come together to eat, wait for one another" (1 Cor. 11:33). If baptism is our inaugurating ceremony into the church, the Lord's Supper is the ongoing ceremony. One is a doorway, the other is the regular family meal. And both proclaim to the nations *who* the people of Christ are.

How does the church exercise its authority of the keys? Through the ordinances. And what, again, is a church? A church is a group of Christians who together identify themselves as followers of Jesus through regularly gathering in his name, preaching the gospel, and celebrating the ordinances. All this they do by the authority of the keys.

What Is a Church?

A group of Christians who jointly identify as followers of Jesus through regularly gathering in his name, preaching the gospel, and celebrating the ordinances.

The Church in Motion

Turning to the rest of the New Testament, we never again hear the words "the keys," but we see them put into motion. The apostles exercise the keys (as in Acts 8:13–23 or 1 Tim. 1:20), as do whole congregations. Never, however, do we see elders or pastors unilaterally excommunicating or readmitting people. (Some point to the call on Titus "to appoint" elders [Titus 1:5], but the word for *appoint* here implies the consent of the congregation.)

In language reminiscent of Matthew 18:20, Paul confronts adultery in the Corinthians church by saying, "When you are assembled in the name of our Lord Jesus with my spirit and with the power of our Lord Jesus, turn that one over to Satan" (1 Cor. 5:4–5). He does not ask the elders to do this behind closed doors. He asks the church to assemble in Christ's name and do this. The concern here, no doubt, is with the *who* of the gospel: who should be called a member and who shouldn't?

There is also a concern with the *who* of the gospel in 2 Corinthians 2:6, where Paul speaks about restoring a man who had been excommunicated from the church "by the majority." A majority supported removing this man from the church, while a minority did not. It's hard to imagine how they determined this apart from a vote.

In Galatians 1, on the other hand, Paul expresses concern over the *what* of the gospel. Speaking to the congregations (not the leaders) of Galatia, he says he is astonished that they are turning to false gospel teachers. They should reject those teachers: "But even if we or an angel from heaven should preach to you a gospel other than what we have preached to you, a curse be on him!" (v. 8). If the gospel is being compromised, gospel-believers outrank an apostle or angel from heaven.

When Should the Church Exercise Its Authority?

Only one question is left in this chapter: when does the church exercise its authority? Surely Jesus did not give churches the keys of the kingdom so that they would bother themselves with photocopier purchases or curtain colors!

The quickest answer is to say that congregations should vote in receiving members and dismissing members (see Matt. 18; 1 Cor. 5), as well as in choosing or removing teachers (see Gal. 1). These are concrete ways to exercise authority over the *what* and the *who* of the gospel.

The larger principle is that working as a priest-king requires members to take responsibility for any decision in which the integrity of the church as a gospel ministry is at stake. Members should surely be involved in changing the statement of faith. How tragic, for instance, when a presbytery announces to a church that "we" (meaning elders and church) have a new definition of marriage. "Really?!" Jesus would have the congregation say. "Maybe *you* do, but *we* don't!" On a more prosaic note, the Bible says nothing about church budgets, but insofar as a church's budget shapes the nature of gospel ministry in a time and place, it may be wise to obtain approval from the church on an annual budget.

To some extent, context will impact which decisions the whole church must make. A fifty-member church with a $100,000 budget may recognize that purchasing a $20,000 church van will impact its ability to pay a pastor and therefore the durability of their gospel ministry. A church with a $4 million budget will not feel this pressure. One church might want to vote on the van, while the other would leave it to the leaders.

The basic principle that should inform where the whole church makes decisions is, does the matter impact the congregation's ability to protect the *what* and the *who* of the gospel? Does it involve the integrity and viability of the church's gospel ministry generally?

When Should the Congregation Vote?

1) In receiving, dismissing, or disciplining members. 2) In selecting elders and deacons. 3) In anything else that significantly impacts the integrity and viability of the church as a gospel ministry.

The Epic Story

We can now put chapter 3's story line together with our elevator ride proof texts, having just unpacked them. Do you see the epic story?

God created you like Adam to be a priest-king, mediating God's own rule through your rule over creation. Yet like Adam you rebelled and cast off God's rule. Salvation came when Christ united you to the new covenant in his blood and granted you his Spirit. You were born again. You repented of your self-rule and followed the second Adam, the King and High Priest Jesus, putting your trust in his perfect life, sin-paying death, and death-defeating resurrection. Jeremiah's promise now applied to you: "No longer will one teach his neighbor or his brother, saying, 'Know the LORD,' for they will all know Me, from the least to the greatest."

In order to be visibly recognized as a follower of Christ and a citizen of his kingdom, you submitted yourself to baptism in a local church, because Jesus has granted such covenanted gatherings of believers the authority to represent heaven's rule on earth. They baptized you into his name, united you to themselves, and publicly re-installed you into Adam's office of priest-king. You therefore joined them in the work of affirming heaven's rule on earth and keeping the temple consecrated to the Lord, which means pronouncing together with the church, "This is a true confession" and "These are true confessors."

You remain accountable to Christ and his people on an ongoing basis through participating regularly in the Lord's Supper, which both declares Christ's death and affirms your membership in the one body, the church. To that end you "examine yourself" while also "recognizing the body" because you know that your job, like a priest, is to protect the line between holy and unholy (1 Cor. 11:28–29; also 2 Cor. 6:14—7:1).

Your membership in the church and participation in the Supper means that, outside the gathering, you wear his Name and that everything you do speaks of him. Like a king, furthermore, you want to conquer territory and bring all things under the rule of God. So you strive to make and build up disciples, living out the gospel in word and deed among fellow believers and unbelieving neighbors.

Such is the life of a priest-king. Such is the work of a church member.

CHAPTER 5

Your Pastors Train You for Your Job

Every member of the church possesses the authority of a priest-king. It's an authority to protect and proclaim the gospel seven days a week. And that authority cannot be trumped even by an apostle or an angel from heaven. So we concluded in the last two chapters.

Still, there is one more question to answer. Remember what you asked me when getting off the elevator back at the beginning of chapter 3? You asked, "What about Hebrews 13:17: 'Obey your leaders and submit to them'?" And it's not just Hebrews. Paul refers to pastors or elders as "overseers" who have been appointed by the Holy Spirit to shepherd the church of God (Acts 20:28). An overseer must oversee, right? And Peter, too, exhorts the elders to "shepherd" and "oversee" God's flock (1 Pet. 5:2). He even tells the young men to "be subject to the elders" (v. 5).

But then the elevator door shut and we couldn't finish the conversation. The basic dilemma was, some Bible passages give authority to the whole assembly. We just spent two chapters looking at them. Other passages, like the ones just mentioned, give authority to the pastors or elders. So how do we reconcile these two kinds of texts? Who's the boss?

This is not just an intellectual exercise. If you are a convinced congregationalist, I hope you are not waiting for me to give you some excuse to get *around* those pastor leadership texts, so that we don't have

43

to pay attention to them. Obeying our leaders, Hebrews 13:17 says, is "profitable" for us. And you and I want to profit! We want what's good for our souls.

If the last two chapters focused on the congregationalism half of Jesus' discipleship program, we come now to the elder-leadership half.

Presbyterians going back to the Reformation have sought to account for both halves by making a distinction between *possession* and *exercise*. The whole church possesses authority, they say, but the leaders exercise it. (The people do exercise authority by electing their leaders; but they cannot remove them.) Presbyterians today still rely on this distinction.

Yet there are at least two problems with this approach. First, if the church can no longer exercise authority after electing the leaders, they don't really possess it. They have been fired. And that means, second, that the members can no longer do the work of a priest-king by protecting the gospel or maintaining the line between holy and unholy. Even if they show up at the office one day, they'll find the locks changed and their keys no good. They might know an elder is a wolf, or that a deacon is a snake, but they will be unable to do anything about it.

There is another way to reconcile these two kinds of texts and explain the relationship between congregational authority and elder authority. We can say that the whole church, elders and members together, possesses the power of the keys. But the elders possess an additional authority to teach and to set the pattern for how the keys should be employed. Instead of a distinction between possession and exercise for comparing congregational and elder authority, we need to distinguish between *possession* and *leading in the use*.

All this together gives us elder-led congregationalism, or Jesus' discipleship program.

Authority of Command, Authority of Counsel

I can explain this distinction between congregational authority and elder authority in three steps. Step one: let me offer you a way of thinking about two different kinds of authority. Try this on for size: we can distinguish between an *authority of command* and an *authority of counsel*.

If you have either kind of authority, you have the right to make commands, and those under your authority are morally obligated to obey your commands (within certain limits). The difference is, someone with an authority of command also has the power to enforce what he or she says; while someone with an authority of counsel does not, but must rely upon the power of the truth itself or upon Jesus to enforce it on the Last Day.

For instance, princes and parents of young children possess what I'm calling an authority of command. By God's design, they have God-sanctioned mechanisms for enforcing their instructions. The prince has what the Bible calls "the sword"; the parent has what the Bible calls "the rod."

Yet we can also think of other authority figures who, in varying degrees, have the ability to give commands that, too, are morally obligating. But they have not been authorized by God to enforce their commands. Think of a husband's authority or a parent once a child reaches a certain age. A husband might instruct his wife, but he cannot enforce his instruction. Either the truth of what he says will enforce itself, or Jesus will enforce what he says on the Last Day.

How is this way of thinking about two kinds of authority useful for the topic of congregations and elders? I think we can say that the congregation, which possesses the keys of the kingdom, has an authority of command. The congregation can enforce its decisions through admitting someone to membership or through excommunication. The pastors or elders, by virtue of their call to teach, have an authority of counsel. They can instruct, warn, rebuke, even command. And their instructions impose some level of moral obligation. Remember, the Holy Spirit has made them overseers (Acts 20:28). And members are told to submit (Heb. 13:17). But nowhere in the New Testament do we witness pastors or elders making unilateral decisions, such as disciplining someone out of a church. Apostles, yes; pastors, no. You, a member, cannot be removed from membership because your pastor says in his office one day, "You're out." Jesus, of course, will enforce an elder's instruction with a wayward member on the Last Day. But the elder cannot.

Those who possess an authority of counsel, like husbands and elders, must continually work to teach and to woo. A godly wife and church member, of course, will require little wooing because each recognizes God's call to submit to husband or pastor. But when points of disagreement arise between wife and husband, or between elder and church member, the husband or elder's only recourse is to woo and to persuade. He cannot pick up "the sword" like the state or "the rod" like a parent. Rather, he must explain himself and seek to instruct. He should not "lord it over" wife or member (Col. 3:19; 1 Pet. 5:3). It may be that the husband or pastor is in error. If he is godly he will be able to hear contrary counsel from wife or member. Yet the fact that God has made the husband or the elder an authority means that he must take the initiative to woo. He cannot force, but neither can he abdicate or give up. Passivity is not an option for him, lest he face Jesus' displeasure on the Last Day. Rather, the husband and pastor must work hard at loving and persuading, equipping and empowering, so that the wife or member *will* choose to follow him in the way of godliness. The authority of counsel, for husband and pastor, must be persistent, patient, long-suffering, tender, affable, consistent, not hypocritical, and, yes, always able to be corrected. It plays for growth over the long run, not forced outcomes in the short run.

Authority to Teach

Here's the second step for understanding the distinction between a congregation's and the elders' authority: insofar as an elder possesses an authority of counsel, not command, it should not be surprising that an elder's authority centers around teaching. That is why an elder must be "an able teacher" (1 Tim. 3:2). Each of the passages mentioned a moment ago involves teaching. In Acts 20, Paul's purpose in calling these elders "overseers" is to remind them that they possess the responsibility to protect the flock against the wolves who "will rise up from your own number with deviant doctrines to lure the disciples into following them" (v. 30). In 1 Peter 5, Peter tells the elders to shepherd and oversee the flock, at least in part, by being an example (v. 3). And in Hebrews 13, the author tells the readers to remember the leaders who taught them God's Word and to imitate their faith (v. 7).

Paul's letters to Timothy and Titus also emphasize teaching. Paul tells Timothy in his first letter to instruct certain people not to teach different doctrines, especially those that promote empty speculation (1 Tim. 1:3–4). Timothy must command and teach (4:11) He must give himself to public reading, exhortation, and teaching (4:13). And he must pay close attention to his life and teaching since that will save himself and his hearers (4:16). Paul then affirms that an elder who rules well is worthy of double honor, especially if his ruling consists of preaching and teaching (5:17). And the elders should teach what Timothy teaches (6:3).

Paul repeats in his second letter to Timothy that Timothy must hold onto the pattern of sound teaching that he has heard from Paul (2 Tim. 1:13). And what he has heard from Paul he should commit to faithful men who will be able to teach others also (2:2). He is to be diligent in correctly teaching the word of truth (2:15). He is to avoid empty speech that deviates from the truth (2:16, 18). And he must teach and instruct only as God would have him teach, knowing that repentance will lead to a knowledge of the truth (2:24–25). Paul concludes by commanding Timothy to preach the Word, to persist in it, correcting, rebuking, and encouraging with great patience (4:2).

Paul opens his letter to Titus by referring to his work of building up people in the truth that leads to godliness (Titus 1:1). He then tells Titus that he left him in Crete to put the church "into order" (1:5 ESV) by appointing elders. Rightly ordered churches have elders who hold firm to the trustworthy word as taught and then give instruction in sound doctrine (1:9). Their opposites always lurk: insubordinate empty talkers who teach for shameful gain (1:10–11). Such individuals must be rebuked (1:13–14). Titus, then, must teach what accords with sound teaching and show himself to be a model of good works (2:1, 7). His teaching must show integrity and dignity so that his message is sound and cannot be condemned (2:8). After reminding Titus of God's salvation, Paul tells him to "Say these things, and encourage and rebuke with all authority" (2:15).

The picture Paul provides for both Timothy and Titus is the slow, patient, day-to-day, repetitious work of seeking to grow a people in godliness. An elder doesn't force but teaches, because a forced act of godliness is no godliness. A godly act is willfully chosen from a regenerate, new covenant heart.

Leading and Training

Third and finally, we should consider what an elder is and does: he is an example for the flock who leads and trains to live like he lives, insofar as he is walking in the way of Christ. Elders do not constitute a separate "class" of Christians, like the division between aristocracy and common folk or between medieval priests and laity. Fundamentally an elder is a Christian and a member of the church. He is set apart and recognized as an elder because his character is exemplary and he is able to teach.

Notice, for instance, that the only qualifications listed for elders in 1 Timothy 3 and Titus 1 not expected of every Christian is that elders cannot be recent converts and they must be able to teach.

In other words, members should not regard elders as possessing "blue blood" (as the aristocracy claimed!) or as having received a special endowment of the Spirit (as medieval priests claimed), two qualities that are out of their reach. Rather, they should regard them as pattern-setters for how they should live and think. They should heed their life and doctrine and imitate them.

The difference between an elder and a member, though formally designated by a title, is based largely in a difference of maturity, not class. Like a parent with a child, the elder constantly works to call the member *up* and *into* maturity. It is a distinct office, to be sure. And not every mature Christian qualifies. Yet the point remains, an elder strives to reduplicate himself in those places where he imitates Christ (see 1 Cor. 4:16; 11:1).

An elder's work is training work. It depends upon modeling and repetition in both word and deed. Speaking figuratively, he demonstrates how to use the hammer and saw, and then places the tools into the member's hands. He plays the piano scale or swings the golf club, and then asks the member to repeat what he has done.

Now think once again of the Presbyterian distinction between possession and exercise mentioned a moment ago. The church possesses authority, they say, but the elders exercise it. What's the problem with this way of relating congregational and elder authority? Besides the fact that it takes possession away from the congregation, depriving them of the work Jesus gave them to do, it stops the elder's work of training! It grabs the hammer and saw and golf clubs back from the member's hands, stopping the repetition. The younger Christians get no training in watching over the *who* and *what* of the gospel. Sorry, kids. Class is canceled.

With elder-led congregationalism, it is always class time. The discipleship doesn't stop. Here are the keys. Drive carefully. Do exactly as I taught you, or you're going to take this thing off the cliff.

Instead of a distinction between *possession of authority* and *exercise of authority*, we need to distinguish between *possession of authority* and *leading in the use of authority*. The whole congregation, elders and members together, possess the keys of the kingdom. But the elders have the task of training, equipping, and leading the congregation to use the keys in a right manner. The congregation possesses and exercises, and the elders show them how.

Ephesians 4 captures this dynamic. Have you ever noticed who does "ministry" in Ephesians 4:11–12. Read carefully: "And He personally gave some to be . . . pastors and teachers, for the training of the saints in the work of ministry, to build up the body of Christ." Who does the work of the ministry and building up the body of Christ? It's the saints! The saints need pastors and teachers to train them. A moment later, Paul says the body "builds up itself in love" as each part does its work (vv. 15–16).

The congregation cannot wisely adjudicate the *what* and the *who* of the gospel—they cannot wisely fulfill their job responsibilities— unless they have gospel teachers teaching and giving oversight. The church needs elders to do their job, just like children need parents and teachers to grow into adulthood. The church needs elders in particular to lead them in the exercise of the keys.

In the vast majority of circumstances, members should submit and follow their leaders. The main time they don't is when the elders or pastors depart from Scripture or the gospel. Assuming godly men lead the church, the vast majority of votes among members in a healthy church should be unanimous and uneventful.

Jesus' Discipleship Program

So now we have come full circle to where we began in chapter 1. Jesus established the leadership of elders and the rule of the congregation as his discipleship program. Remember the formula?

elder leadership **+** congregational rule **=** discipleship

Church members have a job, and pastors train them for their job. The shepherds, who are above reproach and able teachers, establish the pattern of sound living, as well as for guarding the *what* and *who* of the gospel. Want to know how Jesus lives, loves, and walks? Want to know how he keeps his sheep inside the pen and the temple consecrated to the Lord? Watch and listen to these undershepherds.

When the authority of the keys is removed from the church's hands, the ministry of the Word might continue powerfully and fruitfully, but the ministry of application is hindered. No longer do the elders have the opportunity to walk the whole church through "real life" questions of membership and discipline, as discussed in chapter 2. The elders lose a major tool in teaching the congregation how to apply the gospel to real life.

Wielding the keys wisely is a perilous and rocky path. The image that comes to mind is a high crag narrow enough to challenge a mountain goat. The Holy Spirit has given every Christian the competence to hike this path. They can do it. But they also require an able guide: "Place your foot here, not there. That rock won't support your weight. One step at a time. Drink some water. We'll make it." This is the work of the elder. He is an able guide. He leads the way. He says, "This is the way of wisdom. Walk in it" (see Prov. 4:11; 2 John 4; 3 John 3). Only the fool of Proverbs refuses his counsel.

Conclusion

The best definition for elder-led congregationalism, I said in chapter 1, is your pastors training you to do your job. Elder leadership and congregational rule provide a field for training.

Surely members should oppose elders whenever they contradict the Scriptures or demand something beyond the scope of biblical gospel ministry. The congregation always maintains one hand on the emergency brake for such occasions. But hopefully this is a rare occurrence. If elders are leading well, most decisions should enjoy something close to unanimity.

God has given pastors or elders to the church for the church's good. They are a gift (Eph. 4:8–11). A member who refuses to heed the biblical leadership of the elders undermines his or her own discipleship to Christ. Christian growth occurs best as we follow, imitating those who imitate Christ. And the member who learns to follow, often, will soon find himself leading. Just ask Jesus!

Your Job Responsibilities

Jesus' discipleship program gives every church member a job. And this book, I said in chapter 1, is like a church job manual. So now you are wondering, what responsibilities come with this job?

There are at least seven.

Job Responsibility #1: Attend Church Regularly

You, as a baptized Christian and ordinary member of a church, are responsible to attend church regularly. Scripture could not be clearer about this fundamental responsibility so that you can give yourself to love and good works and encouragement.

> And let us be concerned about one another in order to promote love and good works, not staying away from our worship meetings, as some habitually do, but encouraging each other, and all the more as you see the day drawing near. (Heb. 10:24–25)

The author threatens final judgment if you do not attend. The stakes are high indeed. After all, if you do not attend, you cannot fulfill the next six responsibilities. Attendance makes everything else possible.

Job Responsibility #2: Help Preserve the Gospel

You, as a baptized Christian and ordinary member of a church, are responsible for protecting and preserving the gospel and the gospel's ministry in your church.

Think about Paul's "amazement" in Galatians 1: "I am amazed that you are so quickly . . . turning to a different gospel." (v. 6). He upbraids not the pastors, but the members, and tells them to reject even apostles or angels who teach a false gospel.

What this means, Christian, is that you are responsible to study the gospel and know it. Can you explain the gospel to me in sixty seconds or less? Can you explain the relationship between faith and works? Can a Christian live in unrepentant sin? Why or why not? Why is it important for a Christian to affirm the doctrine of the Trinity? What role do good deeds, fellowship, and hospitality play in promoting a church's gospel ministry? Why should a church never let its identity and ministry be subverted by a political party?

These are the kinds of questions, Christian, that you are responsible to answer in order to help guard the gospel. I am not telling you to find answers independently of your elders. They should equip you to answer such questions. If they aren't, you might not be in the best church.

Know the gospel, and what the gospel requires in the church's and a Christian's life.

Job Responsibility #3: Help Affirm Gospel Citizens

You, as a baptized Christian and ordinary member of a church, are responsible for protecting the gospel and the gospel's ministry in your church *by* affirming and disaffirming gospel citizens.

As we saw earlier, Paul doesn't address the Corinthian elders in a matter of discipline, but the Corinthian church itself. Likewise, it is your responsibility, Christian, to receive and dismiss members. Jesus has given it to you. For you to neglect this work only cultivates complacency, nominalism, and eventually theological liberalism.

Of course, the job here is bigger than showing up at members' meetings and voting on new members. It involves working to know and be known by your fellow members seven days a week. You cannot affirm and give oversight to a people you don't know, not with integrity anyhow. That does not mean you are responsible to know personally every member of your church. We do this work collectively. But look for ways to start including more of your fellow members into the regular rhythm of your life. Paul offers a useful checklist for doing this: "Show family affection to one another with brotherly love. Outdo one another in showing honor. Do not lack diligence; be fervent in spirit; serve the Lord. Rejoice in hope; be patient in affliction; be persistent in prayer. Share with the saints in their needs; pursue hospitality" (Rom. 12:10–13). How are you doing on this list?

Job Responsibility #4: Attend Members' Meetings

So how do you preserve the gospel and affirm gospel citizens? By showing up consistently for members' meetings.

Different churches make decisions in different ways, which is fine. But whatever venue your church uses for making the decisions concerning the *gospel what* and the *gospel who*, you should be there.

You cannot do your job if you don't show up to the office.

Admittedly, members' meetings have a bad rap. I understand. So many are unhealthy cauldrons of dispute and insurgency. But don't let bad marriages cause you to give up on marriage. By God's grace, I have been a part of several churches now where the members' meetings feel like warm, encouraging, and engaging family gatherings. Part of that depends on the leadership of the pastors in those meetings and how they plan it. Part of that depends on you.

Job Responsibility #5: Disciple Other Church Members

You, as a baptized Christian and ordinary member of a church, are responsible for protecting the gospel and the gospel's ministry in your church *by* discipling other church members.

Remember Ephesians 4:15–16. The church builds itself up in love as each part does its work. You have work to do to build up the church. And part of that includes the ministry of words. A few verses later, Paul says, "Speak the truth, each one to his neighbor, because we are members of one another" (v. 25). Speak truth to them, and help them to grow. Our words should be "good for building up someone in need, so that it gives grace to those who hear" (Eph. 4:29). Also, make yourself available to be spoken to. Are you willing to listen?

Basic Christianity involves building up other believers. It is a part of fulfilling the Great Commission and making disciples. Speaking of . . .

Job Responsibility #6: Share the Gospel with Outsiders

If Christ has reinstated you as a priest-king, your whole life should reflect the gospel in word and deed. You are an ambassador. Paul's charge and example is worth repeating here: "He has committed the message of reconciliation to us. Therefore, we are ambassadors for Christ, certain that God is appealing through us. We plead on Christ's behalf, 'Be reconciled to God'" (2 Cor. 5:19b–20).

Every Christian has been reconciled, and therefore every Christian has received this message of reconciliation. Therefore, we plead and we pray for sinners to be reconciled to God.

This, too, is a part of your job. The command to "Go and make disciples" belongs to you (Matt. 28:19).

Job Responsibility #7: Follow Your Leaders

It's the job of the pastors or elders to equip the saints for the work of ministry: for these previous six responsibilities. If elders aren't teaching the gospel, catechizing the church in the gospel, teaching them their responsibility for one another, they're ill-equipping the church for the job that Jesus has given them.

Christian, this means that you are responsible to avail yourself of the elders' instruction and counsel. Hold on to the pattern of sound teaching you have learned from your elders (2 Tim. 1:13). Follow their teaching, conduct, purpose, faith, love, and endurance, along with their persecutions and sufferings (2 Tim. 3:10–11).

Be the wise son or daughter in Proverbs who takes the path of wisdom, prosperity, and life by fearing the Lord and heeding instruction. It is better than jewels and gold.

Conclusion

Elder-led congregationalism gives final authority and therefore responsibility to the gathered congregation. With authority comes responsibility.

By joining a church, therefore, you become responsible for what your church teaches and for every single member's discipleship.

- You are responsible to act if Pastor Ed begins to teach a false gospel.
- You are responsible to help ensure Member Candidate Chris adequately understands the gospel.
- You are responsible for Sister Sue's discipleship to Christ, and that she's being cared for and nurtured toward Christlikeness.
- You are responsible to ensure that Member Max is excluded from the fellowship of the church if his life and profession no longer agree.

Who trains you for all this work? Your elders. Add your responsibilities together with theirs and you have Jesus' discipleship program.

When people come to join my church, they are asked to do an interview with an elder, where they are asked about their testimony and to explain the gospel. At the conclusion of any interviews that I personally conduct, assuming that I am going to recommend someone for membership to the whole congregation, I will say something like the following:

> Friend, by joining this church, you will become jointly responsible for whether or not this congregation continues to faithfully proclaim the gospel. That means you will become jointly responsible both for what this church teaches, as well as whether or not its members' lives remain faithful. And one day you will stand before God and give an account for how you used this authority. Will you sit back and stay anonymous, doing little more than passively showing up for 120 minutes on Sundays? Or will you jump in with the hard and rewarding work of studying the gospel, building relationships, and making disciples? We need more hands for the harvest, so we hope you'll join us in that work.

How about you? Have you undertaken this work?

Quick Answers to Critiques of Elder-Led Congregationalism

In this book, I have not tried to defend elder-led congregationalism from its elder-rule, Presbyterian, or Episcopalian model critics. For that kind of apologetic, see my book *Don't Fire Your Church Members: The Case for Congregationalism* (Nashville, TN: B&H Academic, 2016). Below, however, you will find a super short version of some of the arguments in that book.

Common criticisms of congregationalism include:

Congregationalism leads to isolation and fragmentation between churches. It harms the unity that Jesus intended for his church (e.g., John 17:11, 21–23; Eph. 4:1–6).

First, Christians should indeed be united in their obedience to Christ's rule, but there is nothing in any of the biblical-unity texts to suggest that Jesus or the New Testament authors had earthly institutional authority in mind. Maybe they did, but one has to impose that assumption on the unity-texts.

Second, "visible" unity does indeed present an attractive witness to the world. But it's hardly a bishop reaching his hand into a church that the world finds compelling, or the bureaucratic unity produced down at denominational headquarters. The world is compelled when Christians visibly love one another as Christ has loved them, particularly across the generational, ethnic (Jew and Gentile), gender (male and female), political-class (slave and free), education (Greek and barbarian), and general socio-demographic boundaries that divide them (see John 13:34–35; 1 Cor. 12:13–14; Eph. 2:11–22). Loving unity amidst diversity is compelling.

Third, the wonderful illustrations of the interdependence between congregations in the New Testament are not grounded in forced obedience, but voluntarily-given love (e.g., 2 Cor. 8:1–8, esp. 8: "I am not saying this as a command. Rather . . . I am testing the genuineness of your love.").

Fourth, with the exception of the Roman Catholic Church, every tradition engages in splits: Presbyterians dividing from Presbyterians, Anglicans from Anglicans, Lutherans from Lutherans, Methodists from Methodists. What's more, the more logically (and biblically) consistent position is either the Roman or the congregational position, not something in between. Rome is consistent because it says all particular churches should be united in *faith* (gospel belief) and *order* (institutional authority), and it acts accordingly. Congregational churches are consistent because they say all particular churches should be united in *faith*, but *not in order*. Order unites only the local church. Everyone else pleads the importance of unity in faith and order, but then they contradict this claim by uniting only with their own tribe of churches, no more united to churches in other traditions than congregational churches are. The question is, does the unity between local churches called for by the New Testament include institutional order or not? If so, Rome is right, and these churches are being disobedient by dividing from one another. If not, the congregational churches are correct, and these churches deny the authority that belongs to their own members.

For more on unity, see my chapter on church unity in *Baptist Foundations*.

*Congregationalism leads to doctrinal and moral chaos
since there is no higher accountability. After all, who keeps a
congregation accountable?*

The critique cuts both ways, or every way! Who keeps the presbytery accountable? Or the general assembly, the bishop, the synod, or pope? One could easily argue, furthermore, that connectional denominations, in which authority resides outside the local church, have a poorer track record of remaining faithful to Scripture. Just consider Rome and its departure from biblical fidelity that prompted the sixteenth-century Protestant Reformation, or the mainline Protestant denominations, some of which challenge or even outright deny biblical authority. And when the connection becomes unfaithful, every church becomes infected. When a congregational church becomes unfaithful, however, the sickness is relatively contained.

Furthermore, we should learn our church government from the Bible, but it is worth noting how most political thinkers—like the early American founders—knew that political accountability works best when authority is pushed downward, not upward to the king. Should we make the U. S. government accountable by putting it under the United Nations?

The Bible explicitly gives authority to elders (e.g., 1 Tim. 5:17; Heb. 13:7, 17). It does not explicitly give authority to congregations.

First of all, Matthew 18 explicitly authorizes congregations. There is nothing in the text to recommend reading "church" as elders, and there are several reasons not to (e.g., the numeric trajectory of verses 15 to 17; how the original readers would have understood the term "church"). Second, Paul, remarkably, treats the congregations to whom he writes as equals. In 1 Corinthians, he says he has already passed judgment over the sinner (5:3), and then he calls the church to do the same (vv. 4–5; 12). So in Galatians 1 and elsewhere.

For more on the congregation's authority, see chapter 4 in this book and in *Don't Fire Your Church Members*.

Doesn't Acts 15 present a precedent for a council of leaders exercising authority over multiple churches?

A couple things are worth observing in Acts 15. First, the apostles were present, and they claimed the Holy Spirit agreed with their decision. Second, Luke's primary purpose in the passage isn't to establish guidelines for polity, but to explain what the early church determined regarding circumcision and its role in salvation and church membership. They were asking, do I have to become a Jew to become a Christian?

So consider: is the letter from Jerusalem binding on churches *today* by virtue of the authority of the church in Jerusalem, or by its inclusion in Scripture? The answer to that question will indicate what kind of authority the letter sent from Jerusalem bore—ecclesiastical or uniquely apostolic.

Unless you want to argue that the Jerusalem church is institutionally connected to your church (as Rome does), it's a lower bar to say Acts 15 offers no real instruction for church polity. Instead the Holy Spirit-inspired, apostle-written letter that went out from the church in Jerusalem should be treated almost like any other New Testament epistle. It's not binding as a matter of ecclesiological authority, but as authoritative apostolic instruction to eventually be canonized as Holy Spirit-inspired, apostolic Scripture.

For more on Acts 15, see chapter 6 of *Don't Fire Your Church Members.*

Congregationalists merely give lip service to elder authority. They make his leadership advisory.

The critique treats authority as one kind of thing, when the Bible establishes several kinds of authority in the church, all of which work together. Elder authority, in the congregationalist conception, is real authority because (1) God established it (e.g., Acts 20:28); (2) it possesses a heavenly and eschatological sanction, meaning, Jesus will condemn unlawful acts of disobedience to elder authority on the last day; (3) that end-time sanction should weigh upon a believer's conscience; and (4) a pattern of unrepentant insubordination to the elders is potentially grounds for church discipline. For more on elder authority, see chapter 5 of both this book and *Don't Fire Your Church Members*.

Congregationalism is inefficient and makes it hard to get things done.

Compared to other forms of church government, yes, congregationalism can be inefficient. But so is sanctification. The inefficiency of congregationalism is, in essence, the inefficiency of Christian growth. Learning in general is inefficient. Like a parent, a pastor's job is not just to make decisions, but to teach members to make good decisions. And, yes, that takes slow, careful shepherding work. A person who doesn't have patience for that probably shouldn't pastor. Business might be a good career!

Congregationalism is just a reflection of Western democracy. It's a modern idea, not a biblical one.

First, democratic mechanisms were commonly used in the ancient world—everywhere from ancient Greece, to the Roman republic, to the Jewish communities at Qumran. Second, congregational inflections can be heard both in the early church (from the Didache, to Clement, even to Cyprian) and the Reformation church (see Luther and Calvin). Third, the renewal of contemporary forms of congregationalism (1500s) preceded the renewal of contemporary forms of democracy (1700s). Fourth, congregationalism, properly understood, is not a democracy, but a mixed government.

For more on the history of congregationalism and democratic mechanisms in the ancient world, see chapter 4 of *Don't Fire Your Church Members*.

There is no example of every member voting in the Bible.

Yes, there is. Look at what most commentators say about the word *majority* in 2 Corinthians 2:6. What the Bible actually never shows is a session, presbytery, synod, or college of cardinals voting because of course *those aren't in the Bible!* (Every form of polity employs some set of parties voting. It's just a question of whom.)

Finally, voting is a "form," not an "element," meaning there is some flexibility here for context. Churches can make decisions by consensus as well, another mechanism or form.

Congregationalism lets the sheep fire the shepherd (as with Jonathan Edwards). That doesn't make any sense!

Then Paul doesn't make sense, because that's what Paul does. He tells the churches of Galatia to fire him or an angel from heaven for preaching a false gospel (Gal. 1:6–9). This doesn't mean congregations can fire their pastors whenever they please. They need biblical grounds. Jonathan Edward's congregation was probably wrong to fire him, even if they possessed the right to fire him. Legitimate mechanisms can be used wrongly.

"Sheep" don't have authority.

True, but citizens can (see Eph. 2:19; Phil. 3:20; Heb. 8:11, esp. in HCSB). And "sheep" is just one metaphor for church members. Don't overtax it.

Congregationalism is just mob rule, especially when they start to vote on everything!

Yes, in its most unhealthy forms. And Presbyterianism and Episcopalianism are tyrannical . . . in their most unhealthy forms. Every system has its unhealthy versions. For the sake of faithfulness, we should always ask, "What's biblical?" For the sake of fairness, we should assess other systems by their healthy examples, not their unhealthy ones.

And congregations shouldn't vote on everything! For more on where congregations vote, see chapter 4 of both this book and *Don't Fire Your Church Members*.

Congregationalism leads to dictatorship and cult of personality.

As in the last question, this is another (and the opposite) unhealthy form of congregationalism, and every polity has its unhealthy possibilities. The problem here is not the congregation, but the leader. A pastor's job is to disciple and train up other leaders—replacements even—so that a plurality of pastors or elders might lead the church. When a pastor allows his congregation to invest their hopes in him and not God's Word, and when he fails to empower others with authority, he fails to be a Christlike shepherd.

The whole church could not have met in one place in the cities of the ancient Mediterranean.

The multi-thousand member church of Jerusalem did (Acts 2:46; 5:12; 6:2). They even held a members' meeting to discuss church structure (6:2).

Congregationalism fosters infighting and gives immature believers influence.

Perhaps, but you cannot make an omelet without breaking eggs. It's the very opportunity to make decisions that provides a platform for maturity and growth. Congregational rule gives the immature members the opportunity to exercise their "submission muscles" by learning to submit to elder leadership as well as their "wisdom and discernment muscles" by working to protect the gospel. Elder leadership provides the coaching they need. Elder-ruled polities, on the other hand, deny the congregation this opportunity for training and growth.

For more on training immature members, see chapters 1 and 2 of this book.

Congregational rule does not protect the gospel or doctrinal faithfulness because the congregation is not theologically trained or ordained.

The Holy Spirit needs no training, and the Holy Spirit indwells every member of the congregation. Therefore every member should be competent with a basic knowledge of the gospel. To deny this is to deny the promises of the new covenant (see Jer. 31:33–34). Plus, congregational rule does not deprive the congregation of elder leadership. Finally, connectional denominations arguably have a worse historical track record than congregational churches of lurching toward liberalism.

The Bible consistently presents the model of a single leader: Adam, Abraham, Moses, David, and Jesus.

First of all, no, it doesn't. Think of Moses' counselors, or the priest and prophets' check on the king, or the plurality of elders in churches. Second, consider, who is Adam? He is Everyman. He represents all. And who is Christ? The second Adam and Everyman (Rom. 5:12–18). They had unique work to do, but both presented a pattern of rule for humanity. Only one succeeded, and now he has called a new humanity to reign with him forever.

The Bible does not present any one form of church government.

To make this critique, one must show how the different emphases of different texts are contradictory and not complementary parts of a larger picture. I am not sure how you could demonstrate that. There are a few unique historical redemptive factors, like the office of apostles, but I am unaware of any text that doesn't fit the picture of elder leadership and congregational rule.

The larger problem with this critique is, it treats the Bible like a book of Greek political philosophy. It goes looking for an Aristotle-like discussion of the three different models of government. The Hebrew mind, however, was concerned more with the proper nature of relationships (are they holy and just?) and whom God has authorized to do what. If you simply ask this latter question, you will find the Bible's form of church government.

If polity is so clear in the Bible, why are there so many opinions about it?

For the same reason there are many opinions on every area of doctrine: we are finite and fallen. Plus, the topic of church government involves power structures, which means it will be especially contested. The solution is not to deny that the Bible addresses government, but to work harder in asking what Scripture says.

Congregationalism is a static model that does not allow for cultural adaptation.

That is like saying biblical preaching or the Lord's Supper are static and do not allow for cultural adaptations. In one sense, that's true. These elements are universal. But they can adopt different forms in different contexts.

SCRIPTURE INDEX